FEAR NOT!

ANGELS HAVE YOUR BACK

DR. RICK HERTLESS

WITH JOHN ROSE

Fear Not! Angels Have Your Back

ISBN-13: 978-0-9981829-2-6

Printed in the United States of America

RevMedia Publishing

PO BOX 5172, Kingwood, TX 77325

Unless otherwise noted, all Scripture references are taken
from the New King James Version, Thomas Nelson Publishing
Company, Nashville, TN © 1980. Used by permission.

TABLE OF CONTENTS

Chapter One

Human Angels

At the start of this book I need to make it clear that I believe in angels. They are awesome creatures that are servants of God. More than that, I believe in the Creator of the angels, Jesus Christ. John 1:1-14 says:

In the beginning was the Word, and the Word was with God, and the Word was God. He was with God in the beginning. Through him all things were made; without him nothing was made that has been made. In him was life, and that life was the light of all mankind. The light shines in the darkness, and the darkness has not overcome it. There was a man sent from God whose name was John. He came as a witness to testify concerning that light, so that through him all might believe. He himself was not the light; he came only as a witness to the light. The true light that gives light to everyone was coming into the world. He was in the world, and though the world was made through him, the world did not recognize him. He came to that which was his own, but his own did not receive him. Yet to all who did receive him, to those who believed in his name, he gave the right to become children of God—children born not of natural descent, nor of human decision or a husband's will, but born of God. The Word became flesh and made his dwelling among us. We have seen his glory, the glory of the one and only Son, who came from the Father, full of grace and truth.

Jesus is not an angel; although he is called the angel of Lord on occasion which we will discuss later. He is the Creator of the universe. Everything that is made has been made by Jesus. He is not the brother of Satan as some try to say nor was he merely a man. He was not half man half God. He was fully God and fully man and now sits t the right hand of the Father.

As I write this book I am sitting in the hospital waiting room waiting for my dad to have a procedure on his heart. It is a dangerous procedure and before the completion of this book I will know the outcome.

As humans, we live in the physical part of a spiritual world. Most would believe that it is the other way around. But we live in the temporary world; the true world will be that of eternity with God or without him depending on the one you choose.

Partly because of what I am experiencing now and partly because of the topic of this book, I want to share a story with you that happened about 30 years ago.

My dad has had heart trouble most of his life. About thirty years ago he had a stroke. He was in the hospital room in a coma and I was sitting with him while mom stepped out for a moment. All of a sudden he opened his eyes; naturally, I thought he was waking up.

As he began to talk to me I returned conversation, or so I thought, but what he said made no sense. He said, "Don't let the door close." I looked over at the door, but it was not open. I told him, "Dad, the door is not open." He repeated, "Don't let the door close." Once again I looked at the door and reassured him that the door was not open.

But adamantly, with more emotion, he stated, "Please, don't let the door close." I tried to reassure him but he was unrelenting. As he began to point and become more animated he said, "I have to go through the door; it's beautiful there." As I turned to once again look at the door he continued talking, "Its beautiful there, mom and Susan are there and they want me to come with them."

I began to shudder because I began to understand what he was talking about. He continued, "It's the most beautiful place I have ever seen; the grass is so green and they are waiting for me by the river. I must go through the door."

I began to understand because his mom and sister, Susan, had already passed away. Dad was looking into paradise and desired to go to that beautiful place.

This life we live in is temporary. It is but a fleeting moment in our existence. This is a training area for us to make the choice to follow God or deny him. As with all of his creatures,

Angels and humans, we have a free will choice. God gives us this time in our lives to make the decision to follow or reject his goodness and love.

Strangely, there are people who reject God even though they see and understand the majesty of his creation. Stranger than that, the Angels have been in the presence of God in the Throne room, but one-third still decided to leave the glory of heaven by following the Deceiver, Satan.

Angels, like God, are spiritual beings. Actually, man is a spiritual being as well. God created man in a physical body, but he gave us a spirit to be able to converse with God. Ultimately, after the zero to 120 years or so we are granted in this life end, we will live as spiritual beings in an eternity either with God in a place called heaven or apart from him in place called Hell. There are only two choices.

Back to my story; Dad was given a look into paradise; a look at where he would begin eternity. As I began to understand what was happening, I told Dad selfishly, "Let the door close." I was not ready for dad to leave. I told him again, "Let the door close." He repeated, "I want to go through the door, it is beautiful there and I want to see mom." I grabbed his hand and said, "Dad, don't go through the door. Stay here with me; let the door close!"

He started to talk again, "The door is closing." I reiterated, "Let the door close." Sadly he said, "The door is closing." He paused, "The door is closed." At that moment he snapped out of his coma and looked at me. He said, "oh, Hey kid!" Then he fell asleep. I knew that I had him back.

He was out of the hospital three days later as good as he ever was. It was a miracle; it was God. In this miracle, God gave me a glimpse of paradise through the eyes of my Dad. I was privileged to be a part of it.

God has given us the privilege of being a part of the times we are in right now. The eminent return of Jesus is being experienced today. He has given you the privilege to fight the battle alongside side of his Angels.

There is another type of angel I want to briefly address; human angels. As we have been in and out of the hospital with dad these past few months, I have witnessed firsthand another type of servant that I believe is a servant of God; Doctors and Nurses. These are people who are doing a very stressful job but, for the most part, do it with a smile on their face. The job they do can involve some distasteful duties, but they do them nonetheless.

These angels, doctors and nurses, have been given a servants heart by God. That is not to say that they are all going to be in heaven. It is to say, however, that I believe they have been called by God to do the job they do. Each person has to accept Christ, but I believe these angels have a leg up to be able to know more about the true and living God.

As I speak with many of them, they know about the existence of God. Many are professing Christians; all seem to know that what they do is beyond their own capacity to serve. In other words, they see the supernatural on a daily basis.

The Bible says that our battle is not flesh and blood, but with principalities and powers. I wrote the first part of this chapter yesterday. I wrote the second part today. My father has come out of his surgery. Let me help you to understand the magnitude of the danger of this surgery.

First, it needs to be stated the kind of man Dad is. Approximately 35 years ago he was given 6 months to live. Since then, he has had two open heart surgeries, one stroke, four or five heart attacks, 27 or 28 heart catheters, and the surgery he had today. He only had 20% operation of his heart and they were not certain he could withstand any more procedures. Nevertheless, it was a last resort; or lose him.

We all stood in his room, including the doctors and nurses on some occasions and asked God to heal our Dad and/or to give us peace about the decision God would make. The doctors and nurses came in to prepare him and take him away; he was peaceful and in good spirits.

The story has a happy ending. God used his angels to heal my dad. One of the nurses told us that we were "lucky." One of the best surgeons that had ever been at the hospital would work on my dad. I don't believe in luck; I believe in providence. I believe God knew what we were going to pray and placed the best surgeon for the job at this time.

Praise be to God for his majesty! I must take a few moments to stray from the subject of angels. Even though I believe doctors and nurses are God's angels, I believe more in the power of a healing God. I believe and have witnessed the miraculous healing power of God in my life and will continue to do so as I lift him up and pray for the sick.

God may use doctors and nurses, but I believe we should come to him to heal us first, not as a last resort. Many turn to him after they have exhausted what the doctors can do. NO! Come to God first. No matter how small or large the hurt or problem, God cares about you. No matter whether it is money problems, health problems, family problems, addiction problems, or any problem, God says he cares.

James 5:13-16 says:

> *Is anyone among you in trouble? Let them pray. Is anyone happy? Let them sing songs of praise. Is anyone among you sick? Let them call the elders of the church to pray over them and anoint them with oil in the name of the Lord. And the prayer offered in faith will make the sick person well; the Lord will raise them up. If they have sinned, they will be forgiven. Therefore confess your sins to each other and pray for each other so that you may be healed. The prayer of a righteous person is powerful and effective.*

God cares about you. Sometimes he may use his angels to minister to you. Other times, he may simply touch you so you can feel his awesome power. However he decides to touch you, trust him!

As we go through this book we will examine many common and supernatural issues to deal with humans and angels. But the most important aspect of this writing is for you to understand the awesome power of God. He has sent his Son to walk on this earth; to die and be raised to life on the third day; to go to heaven and send us a powerful comforter named the Holy Spirit so that you might walk in peace to be able to share the greatest power in the universe; the gift of salvation in Jesus.

CHAPTER TWO

The Most Beautiful Angel

He was the model of perfection, full of wisdom and perfect in beauty. He was adorned by precious stones: ruby, topaz and emerald, chrysolite, onyx and jasper, sapphire, turquoise and beryl. His settings were made of gold. God made them special for him. He was exalted above all.

He was not only wise; he was "full" of wisdom. There could be no more that could be added. He was blameless and walked among the fiery stones, the precious stones and was given supernatural power over the Kingdom of God.

Even with, literally, all of riches of the universe he defied God and lost everything. He decided that he could be God. He decided that he was better than the Creator of the Universe and opposed the majesty of the Father. He committed the ultimate sin; pride. Not the kind of pride a father might have for a son or a citizen might have for his country; it was the kind of pride that says I am better than anyone. It is the kind of pride that declares it to be the best no matter who it might hurt.

Perhaps you have recognized this to be the description of Satan. What better way to start a book about angels than to begin with the perfect angel? Satan was created perfect, but he had the freewill to choose. He chose unwisely. Strangely, the wisest being every created chose unwisely. Maybe it correlates with the wisest man ever created, Solomon.

Solomon had the world at his fingertips, but he chose to live in anguish. In Ecclesiastes he said, "Everything is meaningless." Everything is meaningless without God. Without being led by the power of God one walks aimlessly in a meaningless existence.

The same can be said for Satan. He walks around aimlessly, seeking whom he may devour (1 Peter 5:8). Satan has nothing to look forward to except a life of eternal torment. His soul purpose is to bring as many with him to destruction as is possible.

Without love, every existence is meaningless. Solomon had 700 wives and 300 concubines (1 Kings 11:3). A concubine is a slave used for sexual purposes. The wisest man in the world had polygamous relationships that led to an unfulfilling life for King Solomon. In Proverbs 5:18 Solomon said, "rejoice in the wife of your youth." Solomon knew the perfect order of God, but he strayed and followed his own wisdom.

It was the same with Satan. God gave him everything, but instead, he became proud and arrogant. He decided he could be better than God. He rebelled and was thrown out of heaven. He rejected God. Some have asked, "Why did God not forgive Satan?" The answer is, when one knows the truth, but then rejects God there is no more forgiveness of sin. Satan walked with God; he talked with him and served him. There was no doubt that he knew God to the fullest. Therefore, the decision was made with full knowledge to rebel against God. God cannot allow evil into his heaven.

Wisdom comes from the Creator and can only be truly accessed by communication with him. When one strays from the wisdom of God, natural wisdom takes over which leads to one's demise. Hebrews 6:4 is clear when it says, "It is impossible for those who have once been enlightened, who have tasted the heavenly gift, who have shared in the Holy Spirit . . . if they fall away, to be brought back to repentance."

How much more enlightened can one be than to actually stand in the presence of God on a daily basis. Satan was the most powerful angel in heaven. He held the greatest stature. It is even been said that he was the worship leader of heaven. One could not have a higher position than to be the leader of praise to a great and mighty God.

Nevertheless, when he was thrown from heaven he was stripped of his power. Satan is not one to be feared by the Christian. In fact, James 4:7 says, "Submit yourselves, then, to God. Resist the devil, and he will flee from you." Did you get that? Submit to God! Follow God and there is no fear of anything in heaven or in earth.

At the time of writing this book my Dad is in the hospital. I stopped by to see him today. He said that Satan placed a thought in his head and his heart filled with fear. That is one way to discern if God or Satan is speaking; God invokes peace and comfort, Satan invokes fear and distress. He told me he said the simplest of prayers to God and his peace enveloped him. Resist the devil and he must flee (James 4:7).

Satan is the Father Lies, the King of Fear, the Deceiver, the Manipulator and any other evil word you can think of. Why would I write about him in chapter two of a book called "Fear Not?" Because it is my desire that you understand the power you have to live a victorious life in Christ. What better place to start than to explain that YOU, who have Jesus in your life, have power over the "most powerful" evil one in the universe.

Did you understand what I just wrote? You have more power than Satan himself if you walk in the power of the Holy Spirit. Romans 8:11 says, "But if the same Spirit that raised Jesus from the dead is living in you, he who raised Christ from the dead will also give life to your mortal bodies through his Spirit who lives in you." Did you get that? He said twice in the same sentence that the most powerful Spirit ever known DWELLS IN YOU! WOW! That is exciting! That should get you to dancing. That should get your blood pumping. Even though this book is to explain some of the duties of the angel of God, FEAR NOT, you have the power of God in you.

Satan is a fallen angel that not only has to submit to God, he has to submit to you if you are washed in the blood of

Jesus. That is not to say that you should wield the power with arrogant pride; that was Satan's sin. However, it is to say that if you rebuke Satan in the name of Jesus and with his authority, he and his demons have to flee. Therefore, it should be stated right at the onset of this book, JESUS HAS YOUR BACK! He has said that you have the power to command Satan and his angels "off the property." Not with timidity, but with authority.

The archangel Michael did not dare rebuke the devil in his own power, instead he said, The Lord rebuke you (Jude 1:9)."

This might be a good time to make clear the position of Satan. Satan is not omniscient (all-knowing), omnipotent (all-powerful) nor omnipresent (everywhere at the same time). He is limited on this earth much the same as you and I. He has to send his minions out. If Satan is influencing or personally agitating someone in the world he has to do it one-on-one as he has time to get to them. Make no mistake, he can travel much faster than you or I, because he is spirit, but he cannot be at many places at the same time. The Father, the Son and the Holy Spirit, on the other hand, are everywhere at the same time. God is all-knowing. He knows what you are going to do before you do it. Satan has to wait until it happens, or hear what your intent is, to know how to react. We hold the advantage because we have the power of the Holy Spirit within us to guide us.

If we will keep in constant communication with God through the Holy Spirit of Jesus, we will be ahead of Satan every step. It is when we get out of communication we get in trouble.

Therefore, stay in communication with God. In other words, pray, read the Bible and go to church. Keep in fellowship with other believers and uphold each other in power.

So, what does all of this mean? Do we need the angels or not? God does nothing in a vacuum. All of his creation has a purpose; yes, even those mosquitoes, scorpions and the like. His angels keep us from having to constantly fight the battle. His angels "watch our back." His angels are messengers and even help to keep us doing what we are supposed to do for the glory of Jesus Christ.

As we go through this book together, we will learn of the awesome love God has for his creation, but none more than his "crowning glory (Psalm 8:5)." Mankind is his greatest creation. Psalm 8:6 said God put everything under man's feet.

Satan is not to be feared; neither is he to be underestimated. If you fight him in the flesh,you will lose. It is only through the power of the Holy Spirit one can win the battle against Satan. That is why Jude warned that the archangel Michael had to rebuke him in the power of God. Angels are not filled with the Holy Spirit.

Man is different from the angels; we are infilled with the Holy Spirit. Plus the translation of Psalm 8:5 says that man was made "a little lower than the angels." However, I submit that this translation "misses the mark." The word used that was translated as angels in the Hebrew is *'elohiym.* The word " *'elohiym*" is also translated as "God." Therefore, a better translation might be, "Man was made a little lower than God." This translation seems to fit better in this context because Man, not angels, is indwelt with the Holy Spirit of God.

Romans 8:17 says, "And if children, then heirs; heirs of God, and joint-heirs with Christ; if so be that we suffer with him, that we may be also glorified together." Jesus is our brother; therefore, we are created a little lower than God makes sense as a translation.

Satan's main power is the power to make us do things against God. He persuaded Eve to eat the fruit and the Adam followed. Satan made Man doubt the validity of what God has promised.

King David had been given a promise in 2 Samuel 7:14. It said, "Your house and your kingdom will endure forever before me; your throne will be established forever." This should have instilled the trust to know that God would have given Israel victory no matter the odds.

In 2 Samuel 21 it says that Satan incited King David to count the troops of Israel. So what's the harm? A leader should know what he has to fight with. No, his counting said that he did not trust God; he wanted to make sure HE had enough troops. The truth is, God is enough! No matter the size of the fighting force. Nevertheless, Man was again fooled by the wise serpent, Satan.

Satan was the chief angel; the angel of angels. Now he is the chief demon. Instead of being the "light bearer" he is the prince of darkness. Angels are God's created beings; they are not people who have died before us. The people in Christ who have died before us are in paradise with Christ. He told the thief on the cross he would be with Jesus in paradise that very day (Luke 23:43).

This means, when a person dies who is in Christ, he or she goes to paradise with Jesus. Is paradise heaven? The Bible is not absolutely clear on the distinction. Nevertheless, when one who is in Christ dies, he goes to a place of peace rather than a place of torment. Possibly, it is a holding place for the return of Christ before we all go to heaven. Even so, that is for the topic of another book.

For the purposes of this study, it is sufficient to say that one goes to live with Christ, not to become an angel. That is not to say that we will have nothing to do in heaven, but our duties will be different from those of the angels.

The angels are not to be feared; that includes Satan. If you have a relationship with Jesus, you have the power within you to overcome the Satan and the world. You have the power within you to defeat the enemy and live the abundant life. Jesus said, "I have come that you might have life and have it more abundantly (John 10:10). Satan comes to kill and to destroy, Jesus came to give life.

If you accept the life of Jesus you will have struggles, but you will be given the power to overcome the struggles. If you choose Satan, your struggles in this world may be few, but eventually, the acceptance of sin will catch up and you will live in an eternity without Christ; an eternity of suffering and torment.

Throughout the rest of this book we will examine and discover the awesome power available to us as Christians. The "trick" is to get up and do something. The world is in chaos because Christians have allowed Satan, "the beautiful one" to infiltrate every aspect of life including the church. The world wants glitz and glamour and in the name of getting people to fill the church, leaders have given in to the glitz and glamour theory.

The truth is, Satan was the "bearer of light," but Jesus is The Light. Satan's glitz and glamour is fleeting, but Jesus' light is forever. Satan offers a temporary "high;" Jesus offers abundance for eternity. Satan is the deceiver; Jesus is the Truth. Satan offers fleeting power over the moment; Jesus offers eternal power to live in love.

The abundant life that Jesus spoke of is real. It is a life that must be shared with others for it to come to true fruition. Christians, it is time to get off of your couch and get into the battle. These are the last days. There are too many signs in the news that prove it. Do not be the one who has decided to sit it out. Do not be deceived, trust God! Embrace the fulfilment of your calling.

Chapter Three

The Most Powerful Angel

As she sat by the spring she contemplated her life. How she had planned for it to be different. As a child her mind ran wild with thoughts of baring many powerful children that would change the world. But now, it seems as though her life is over. She has been cast out into the desert to uncertainty of life. Would she even survive the day? Would she find life in an inhabitance far away?

Her disparity must have been great. She must have been thinking, "My life is over." She was running away to nowhere; to a place far away, but without destination. Her tear soaked cheeks begged the question of her crimes. Not wanting to accept any responsibility she placed the blame solely on those who made her leave the comfort of her home.

Isn't that the human way? Whatever you are facing in your life, do accept any of the blame or is it the other guys fault; better still, is it God's fault? When we face struggles in our life we try to justify them away from ourselves. But truly, most of the blame befalls us if we are to honest.

If we would totally trust God, our lives would be much more ordered, but the Bible teaches us that it is impossible for us to trust God in his entirety. That is why he had to send his Son, Jesus. Strangely, the most powerful angel in the Bible is not an angel at all, but we will discuss that later. Let's get back to our story.

Hagar is the woman in despair. The above scenario was not of "her own" making, but she had much to do with it. Sarai, before she was Sarah, Abram's wife gave her maidservant to her husband to fulfill the promise of the Lord for Abram to be given an heir. Maybe it is best to start from the beginning.

Abram trusted God. He lived in a place called Haran. When he was seventy five years old, God came to him and told him to go to an unknown place. Abram didn't question God; he set out immediately. God said he would make Abram's name into a great nation.

Sarai, Abram's wife, was barren; she could not have children. So, Sarai surmised that if Abram was to have a child, it would have to be provided through her maidservant Hagar. Unfortunately, when Hagar got pregnant she began to claim power she did not have. She must have thought that her stature had been raised because she was to be the mother of Abram's child and not Sarai.

So, Sarai had enough and told Abram she had to go. So as

you can see, much of Hagar's predicament was of her own making. Because of her pride, she "lorded" the pregnancy of Abram's son over Sarai.

But the blame was not solely on Hagar. Abram and Sarai did not believe the Lord and they came up with the plan to fix it. Have you ever done that? God has made a promise, but it wasn't fast enough. So you devise a plan to "help" God. When all is said in done, you are in a bigger mess than when you first started. By the time you trust God you are in a desert by a spring crying because you don't know where to turn.

That brings us back to our story and the Most Powerful Angel. The angel of the Lord appeared to Hagar. She was told to go back to the camp and submit to Sarai. Who is the angel of the Lord? Many believe, as I do, he was Jesus; the pre-incarnate Christ. In Genesis 16:10 it says, "I will increase your descendants . . ." A normal angel has no authority to make such a statement. The normal angel would say something like, "The Lord will increase your descendants . . ." He would not use the personal pronoun "I".

There are other places in the Bible where the "angel of the Lord" is declared as God. Genesis 22:15-16 says, "The angel of the Lord called to Abraham from heaven a second time and said, "I swear by myself, declares the Lord . . ." No common angel can swear by anything other than God.

Why does Jesus appear as an angel? I believe this is the perception because he appears in the flesh. Hebrews 13:2

says, "Be not forgetful to entertain strangers: for thereby some have entertained angels unawares." In other words, you could encounter angels unknowingly from day to day. How you take care of them says something about your character. Perhaps, even Jesus can appear to us as a stranger.

I was asked the question the other day, "Can angels appear to us as an animal?" God, Jesus, the Holy Spirit, angels and demons are spirits. They have no form that must be conformed to for their existence. Humans, on the other hand, are confined to the body given to us by God until we are given our glorified body. Therefore, an angel, or a demon for that matter, could inhabit animals.

Jesus is all-powerful! He can still appear to us today. Matthew 26:64 says, "Jesus replied. 'But I say to all of you: From now on you will see the Son of Man sitting at the right hand of the Mighty One and coming on the clouds of heaven'." How can this be? If he is on the throne, how can he be here as well? Jesus is now Spirit. Unlike Satan, he is God; he is omnipresent. He is everywhere at the same time. He can be in the Throne Room in Heaven as well as my living room.

Jesus came to us in the form of a man, much the same way as he did in the Old Testament as "The angel of the Lord." An all-powerful God can take any shape he so desires. He can also allow his angels to do the same. Plus, Satan is a spirit as well and he and his minions can take on shapes to deceive. The main difference is his power is limited by time. There will come a day when he will no longer be able to deceive the masses. He will be thrown into the Lake of Fire for all eternity. Until then, he is allowed to walk the earth, "seeking whom he may devour (1 Peter 5:8)."

The secret to the above Scripture is that Satan seeks whom he "May" devour. He cannot devour those who are sealed by the Holy Spirit. If you are sealed by the Holy Spirit you are in eternity. If however, you have simply made a gesture to God and then have continued in your sinful life, you are not sealed.

I want to take a few moments to expound on the previous statement. It is important for your everyday walk to understand the security of your salvation. There are some who believe one can lose his or her salvation. I don't believe that. However, it must be stated that one has to be saved in the first place.

Ephesians 4:30 says, "And do not grieve the Holy Spirit of God, with whom you were sealed for the day of redemption." The Scripture is clear that you are sealed by God when you accept his Son. However, for far too long it has been said that all one has to do is confess that Jesus is Lord and he will be saved. There are two parts of the equation; one part is to confess with your mouth and the other is to believe in your heart.

Romans 10:9 says, "If you declare with your mouth, 'Jesus is Lord,' and believe in your heart that God raised him from the dead, you will be saved." Jesus has to be Lord of your life. Even the demons believe in Jesus; and they tremble (James 2:19)! Believing is not enough. One must serve and accept Jesus as

Lord of one's life. In other words, one must trust God and obey his Word.

If there is no change in one's life, he or she is not saved. That is not to say that the saved will not have struggles and face sin in his or her life. But, what is one's pattern?

How do you live your life? Do you try to please God or yourself? Is your main concern Sunday mornings to go fishing or shopping or to go where God is? We are to fellowship with believers if we are his.

If you are sealed by the Holy Spirit, you will want to do as God wants you to do. 2 Corinthians 1:21-22 says, "Now it is God who makes both us and you stand firm in Christ. He anointed us, set his seal of ownership on us, and put his Spirit in our hearts as a deposit, guaranteeing what is to come."

This seal is much like the Mark of the Beast. The Bible says, and it is widely held, that once a person receives the Mark on his right hand or forehead he cannot turn back. He is sealed for all eternity with the devil. Revelation 14:9-10 says:

> *A third angel followed them and said in a loud voice: "If anyone worships the beast and its image and receives its mark on their forehead or on their hand, they, too, will drink the wine of God's fury, which has been poured full strength into the cup of his wrath. They will be tormented with burning sulfur in the presence of the holy angels and of the Lamb. And the smoke of their torment will rise for ever*

and ever. There will be no rest day or night for those who worship the beast and its image, or for anyone who receives the mark of its name."

The Mark of the Beast is eternal for his followers. How much more the seal of the Holy Spirit? Once you have truly accepted Christ and follow him you are saved. All of this is extremely important for understanding the Most Powerful Angel in the Universe, The Angel of the Lord; Jesus Christ.

The angel of the Lord is Jesus in Spirit form. Judges 2:1 says, "The angel of the LORD went up from Gilgal to Bokim and said, 'I brought you up out of Egypt and led you into the land I swore to give to your ancestors. I said, 'I will never break my covenant with you . . ." Again, the angel of the Lord said "I" brought you out of Egypt. Exodus makes it clear that Israel was brought out of Egypt by God. Therefore, the angel of the Lord and the person of the Godhead, Jesus, are one in the same.

The title "The Angel of the Lord" is proof that Jesus is in charge of the angels. It is he who the angels answer to do his will. It is also possible that he might be one of the "angels unaware" the Bible speaks of in Hebrews 13:2.

CHAPTER FOUR

Angels on Assignment

It is a cool morning. The kind that makes you desire the sun and embrace the aroma of the sky. The clouds hang lazily in the calming breeze. You hear the sheep nearby with the gentle "Bah" of normalcy.

Suddenly, your moment is interrupted. The herd seems more agitated than before. The unrest is surrounding the camp of peace. The unrest soon grows to chaos and utter despair is heard from your sheep. Unexpectedly, the chaos stops and a calm returns; but only the calm that animals embrace. Your spirit insists, "Something is not right."

In the quiet of the moment you witness the fruition of your restless spirit. A lion has a sheep in his mouth retreating to the brush; confident that he has acquired his daily meal. Without thought you grab your staff and run toward the danger. As you run you try to devise a plan to retrieve the now frantic sheep, but the plan doesn't come.

Your faith in God has always seen you through situations, but no situation has ever appeared with the danger of this one. Still, your job is to protect your flock. No matter the consequences, you are their only hope.

Running up to the lion you strike him in the back. He is startled and drops the sheep. In his confusion you rescue the sheep and begin to run, but the lion will not give up his meal so easily. He turns and attacks but you step aside and grab his mane; with one fell blow you cut his throat with you knife. The lion falls lifeless and bloody, but you escape unharmed. Saved by the faith you have in God; your Protector.

That must have been one of the scenes of David as he smote the lion to protect his flock. David told the story to King Saul as he made his plea to confront the giant Goliath. 1 Samuel 17:32-36 says:

> *David said to Saul, "Let no one lose heart on account of this Philistine; your servant will go and fight him." Saul replied, "You are not able to go out against this Philistine and fight him; you are only a young man, and he has been a warrior from his youth." But David said to Saul, "Your servant has been keeping his father's sheep. When a lion or a bear came and carried off a sheep from the flock, I went after it, struck it and rescued the sheep from its mouth. When it turned on me, I seized it by its hair, struck it and killed it. Your servant has killed both the lion and the bear; this uncircumcised Philistine will be like one of them, because he has defied the armies of the living God.*

Have you ever been in a situation in which you thought you might have been hurt or even killed? But nothing happened; not a scratch.

It is not clear who the Psalmist of Psalm 91 is, but many were written by King David. Psalm 91:9-13 says:

*If you say, "The LORD is my refuge," and you make the Most High your dwelling, no harm will overtake you, no disaster will come near your tent. **For he will command his angels** concerning you to guard you in all your ways; they will lift you up in their hands, so that you will not strike your foot against a stone. You will tread on the lion and the cobra; you will trample the great lion and the serpent (Bold Italics added).*

God has given angels charge over those who trust in him. In Daniel 10:10 Daniel prayed to God and God sent him help in the form of an angel. The Bible says, "Are not all angels ministering spirits sent to serve those who will inherit salvation? (Hebrews 1:14)." The angels are sent to the Elect to minster to them.

God watches over the little ones. Matthew 18:10 says, "Take heed that ye despise not one of these little ones; for I say unto you, That in heaven their angels do always behold the face of my Father which is in heaven (KJV)."

God cares deeply for his children. It is not his will that any should perish; therefore, he watches over the little one's safety.

Perhaps if you are reading this and have lost a child you might be thinking, "Why did he not watch my child?" He did! He brought the child home to himself early, not wanting the child to experience the hardships that befall those of us who have to endure this life.

God commanded the angels to protect David in the battle with the lion and the bear and, later, Goliath. David trusted God to protect him, but there is one ingredient that goes hand-in-hand with stated protection. You must trust!

Once you lose your trust, you will never chase the lion, the bear, or Goliath. It is up to the Christian to understand that God has your best interests at hand. If you will trust him he will take you to unimagined heights. If the highest you ever go is the step latter, the most you can build is a one story house. But if you will get in the crane, you can build a skyscraper.

At this point you might be thinking, "What about those who have died and are dying? God is not protecting them. The angels are not coming to their aid." Really? God's grace is sufficient for every situation.

In the 1500's there was severe persecution of the church. There was a good possibility that a Christian would be killed and if one was a pastor, it was probable one would die through martyrdom.

Michael Sattler was a pastor during the 1500's. He was arrested for preaching the Gospel by Count Joachim of

Zollern, regent of Archduke Ferdinand of Austria, along with his wife and several other Anabaptists.

Anabaptist simply means re-baptizers. The Catholics believed in infant baptism, but believers believe that the decision is made to accept Christ and then be baptized. This infuriated the Catholics because it basically called there doctrine and papal leadership false.

Sattler and company were members of the Swiss Brethren. In February 1527 he chaired a meeting of the Swiss Brethren at Schleitheim, at which time the Schleitheim Confession was adopted. Within the Confession there were seven articles.

The premise of the articles was to define how the Brethren Church would operate, but the article that intrigued me was #5 – "On pastors in the church of God: . . .But should it happen that through the cross this pastor should be banished or led to the Lord [through martyrdom] another shall be ordained in his place in the same hour so that God's little flock and people may not be destroyed."

Did you recognize that they were preparing for the time the pastor would be martyred? They were ready with another pastor for the impending demise of the then current pastor. Anyway, here is where it gets interesting and relevant to our topic.

When the Christians were being tortured, burned, drowned or otherwise mutilated for the Gospel they would preach. Many came to salvation because those being persecuted would give the Gospel. Therefore, officials began cutting out their tongues so the condemned could not speak. The story goes; Michael Sattler realized that there would come a day when he might face execution. So, he set up a predetermined signal for his congregation. If God's grace was sufficient, even being burned at the stake, he would hold up two fingers.

The time came and Sattler was tortured and burned. As the fire raged, just before he died, he held up two fingers. God's grace is sufficient.

God cares for his children in a multitude of ways. If you know Jesus as Lord and Savior you have been sealed by the promised Holy Spirit. This sealing includes protection, even in the time of death.

At this juncture I believe it is important to remind you; Death Is Not the End!! It is the beginning. Though most fear the unknown, God has placed in the Believers heart the comfort that he will bring you to an eternity that cannot be imagined. 1 Corinthians 2:9 says, "However, as it is written: "What no eye has seen, what no ear has heard, and what no human mind has conceived— the things God has prepared for those who love him— . . ." Paul said to be absent from the body is to be present from the Lord (2 Corinthians 5:8)."

We can trust God with our eternity, but we have a hard time trusting him with our "today." He loved us so much he sent us a Comforter after Jesus left us. I believe, this Comforter, the Holy Spirit should give us more peace of mind and spirit than the angels; mainly because, the Bible says that the same Spirit that raised Jesus Christ from the dead dwells in us (Romans 8:11). I realize I have made this point previously, but I want to restate it in case you missed it.

We have the most powerful entity in the universe within us; it is the Spirit of God himself. If we will understand that power, we will never fear evil again. Evil is of Satan and Satan has to flee if we who are saved, believers in Jesus, command him to. Did you get that?

Angels are awesome! They help us know of the power of God, but we hold a greater power than the angels. We walk in the Spirit of Jesus Christ, we are joint heirs with Jesus and we are sons of God. Wow! That should make you want to shout; get up and dance; put a smile on your face that won't go away.

Yes, there are angels assigned to "watch your back." But once the angels alert you to danger you can take care of it by the power of the Holy Spirit. In fact, it can be said that if you walk in the power of the Holy Spirit, you will discern between the spirits and know they are coming beforehand.

We serve an awesome and powerful God who has given us the resources to call on his name and it is taken care of. If you were the President of the United States' son or daughter, wouldn't you invoke his name if you needed too? One step further, would you even need to invoke his name because powerful people already know who you are by association.

How much more because you are a child of the King. Remember the sons of Sceva? The story is in Acts 19:13-16:

Some Jews who went around driving out evil spirits tried to invoke the name of the Lord Jesus over those who were demon-possessed. They would say, "In the name of the Jesus whom Paul preaches, I command you to come out." Seven sons of Sceva, a Jewish chief priest, were doing this. One day the evil spirit answered them, "Jesus I know, and Paul I know about, but who are you?" Then the man who had the evil spirit jumped on them and overpowered them all. He gave them such a beating that they ran out of the house naked and bleeding.

If you are a child of the King, the evil spirits know it; Satan knows it! You do not have to walk in fear. However, as can be gleaned from the above story, if you are trying to fake your relationship with Christ, you are in danger of being beaten and bloodied.

Angels are some of the most awesome creatures in God's Kingdom, but so are you. Angels are not to be worshipped; they are to be partnered with to defeat the enemy of Christ.

Chapter Five

Angels Are Powerful

As you sit in your cold, damp cell, you ponder the events of the day; maybe even the events of the past few years. Life has been a whirlwind of late, but you have never felt more peace and calm than now.

God has blessed your life in so many ways it is difficult to count. He has allowed you to spread the Gospel around the world and see thousands come to Christ. The miracles performed by your hands have been nothing short of amazing.

Watching the Holy Spirit work with the simple mention of Jesus has been something to behold. People have been healed, delivered and changed by the sound of the name of Jesus Christ. But it has not come without a price. Powerful people have been offended and have plotted for your demise.

They have tried to shut you up; they even killed your friend James. Nevertheless, you continue to proclaim the Good News. Now, you have been arrested and put in prison; waiting for the morrow to proclaim your death sentence. Even so, you have the calm that you have never experienced before.

Death no longer holds fear. No, it brings excitement and victory. Tomorrow you get to go home to live with Jesus for eternity. With that thought you gently fall asleep; a sleep like no other; the deep sleep of satisfaction, not the restless sleep of the condemned.

As you sleep you feel a gentle nudge and believe it is part of your sweet dream. You do not awaken. Then, you feel the kick in your side like that of a close friend telling you to, "Wake up!" As your eyes open you see the bright light filling your cell. You think, "I know this is a dream."

Standing before you is an angel of the Lord telling you to get up. When you do the chains fall off of your ankles and wrists. But you know you are dreaming so you go along with your deliverer quietly. The truth is, you begin to laugh at the scenario, because it can't be true. You think again, "I know this is a dream; it is even sort of comical."

As you follow your deliverer your mind goes to tomorrow on the day you are to be killed and think, "This is the Lord giving me even more peace to ready me for what I must face."

You pass the second and third gate and now you know it is a dream because the guards make no effort to wrangle you into submission. You come to the main gate and it opens automatically. Then you walk into the street and the angel disappears.

At this point you come to your full senses and realize that God has sent an angel to free you from the prison.

This is the scenario found about Peter in Acts 12. The true account of Peter in prison shows the power of the angels who are working on your behalf. Peter was walked through a guarded prison in plain sight, but undetected because of the veil placed over the guards by the angel.

Even though we walk in the power of the Holy Spirit, perhaps the Lord sometimes send his angels to bolster our faith.

You are protected in the very same way. God sends his angels around you constantly to protect you from the fiery darts thrown by the enemy; darts that you don't even know about; darts that you might take for granted.

It could be stated that Americans take too much for granted in our "American Dream." There are people around the world who will be reading this book who don't understand the complacency of Americans or even the West. Europe has taken Christ for granted for years. Now, America is following suite.

Because of the complacency, or in some cases apathy, American is experiencing the withdrawal of the blessings of God. God will not be mocked. Even so, in the past several years it seems as though America has mocked God on a daily basis.

Perhaps you ask, "How have we mocked God?" In the 60's we said we don't need God in our schools. Since then, violence, teenage pregnancy, minimal grade scores and much more has plagued our schools. The church remained silent.

In the 70's we allowed abortion to become the law of the land. Since then we have murdered millions of babies at the altar of convenience. The result is a lower work force to replenish the country, not to mention the sin of the murder itself. The lower work force has resulted in not enough labor to fill jobs which have led to a disastrous economy, poverty and hunger in the streets of America, not to mention the flippant way we have cast human life aside; again, the church remained silent.

In 2009, Obama declared that America was no longer a Christian nation without any reprisal from the church. Once again, the church was content to sit in their auditoriums and cry, "Bless me Lord!"

In 2016, homosexual marriage has been declared the law of the land. America has once again proclaimed that God did not know what he is doing and we can handle this. The church cried out for a total of one week in "outrage." Then, they not only went back to business as usual, but embraced the decision in the name of "inclusiveness." It is time for the church to repent and become the church of Jesus Christ.

Peter and the other apostles proclaimed the Gospel no matter the cost. The angels "had their back." The angels have your back as well, but you have to get in the battle. If you are not willing to fight you will remain in relative security; that is until the battle runs over you.

I was watching "The Patriot" the other day. It is a movie starring Mel Gibson about the American Revolution. In a town meeting, the star of the movie, Benjamin Martin, declined to get into the battle. He said that he wanted to stay out of the fight and keep his family safe. Instead, the battle found his house and one of his sons was killed before his very eyes. Later, he repented to one of his remaining sons because he waited too long to get in the battle which led to losing the first son.

Is that what you're doing? God wants his children to get into the battle. It is ironic to me that America has tried to remove God from every aspect of her existence until a disaster happens. Then everyone says, "Where was God in this?" I'll tell you where he was. He was outside of America allowing her to have what she wanted.

We cannot have it both ways. God wants to be a part of our lives if we will allow him to. But he will not force himself on us. It is his will that none should perish (2 Peter 3:9). Even so, he has given us the plan he has for us to inherit eternal life. John 6:28-29 says, "Then they asked him, 'What must we do to do the works God requires?' Jesus answered, 'The work of God is this: to believe in the one he has sent'."

Do you want to experience the power of angels? Then get in the battle. You will see God in action through these powerful beings that are placed at your disposal.

Did you say you didn't want to see God work through

his powerful angels? Then I say, "Repent!" That is a word that American Christians of the twenty-first century have forgotten. God has not called us to cars, houses, jewelry and material abundance. He has called us to service, proclaiming the Gospel and, if needs be, persecution.

Don't get me wrong. I believe in the abundant life of John 10:10 where Jesus states, "I have come that you might have life and that more abundantly." But the abundance is not to fulfill your lustful desires. It is to further God's Kingdom.

It is a fact that some can handle money better than others; let them give generously to the church. However, the church then must give it to the Kingdom. It is not be stored up in a vault, waiting for a "rainy day." IT IS RAINING NOW!

What does your church give to? Does your church give? What does your budget report look like? I have been a pastor of a few churches and have been in meetings with many churches and pastors. The wealth of the church is stored up in Banks. Churches walk afraid to spend the money for fear they will not have enough to pay next month's bills. Does this sound like trust in God to you? To me it sounds like trust in banks. It sounds like trust in money.

Come out from her you workers of iniquity! The Babylonian system is rampant in our culture. Even the church is polytheistic (believes in many gods). You might ask, "How?" One example has already been stated; the church is more worried about money than the Gospel. Church members desire to hang on to their money in case *THEY* need it. In the book of Acts, the church came together and shared their belongings, food, money and resources so that all might have their needs taken care of (Acts 4). I am not advocating communism by any stretch of the imagination. In fact, it might be said the first church went above and beyond the call. God gave us his financial plan in the book of Leviticus. One tenth of our income should be set aside for the Lord for a start.

I am not going to get into a theological debate about whether or not the tithe was abolished in the New Testament. If anything, God stepped it up. Think about it, in the book of Acts everyone gave everything; just something to think about. Nevertheless, if Christians in America would believe God only for the tenth that is commanded in the Old Testament, the church would be without financial want and would be able to supply every missionary in the world amply.

But for the sake of argument, forget about the tithe. If each member of the church would devise in his heart how much to give and give it faithfully, the churches needs would be met. Instead, many give when they feel like it or when it is convenient. Many members who have ample wealth believe giving $50 a month should be plenty for the church. GOD DESERVES BETTER!

Many of you might say, "I don't trust the church to give the money where I believe it should go." You have a couple of choices; fire the pastor and get one you trust or find a new church to attend. BUT GET IN THE GAME! The "Game" will be won without you, but wouldn't you rather be in the game making a difference?

Perhaps, you might be thinking, "I thought this was a book about angels, not tithing." It is impossible to separate the Word of God. Each subject studied must be balanced with the other. God did not write one book about angels, one about money, one about salvation and one about the end times. He wrote the Bible in the context of how one lives in a normal life. I feel obliged to do the same.

When a preacher talks only about the topic he wants to purport he can get in trouble. Then in kind, those who study under him get in trouble as well. Many cults have been started because there are individuals who focus on one thing and that one thing is usually not Jesus. The study of angels can be such a topic.

There are many people who worship angels. God forbid! Paul writes in Colossians 2:18:

> *Do not let anyone who delights in false humility and the worship of angels disqualify you. Such a person also goes into great detail about what they have seen; they are puffed up with idle notions by their unspiritual mind.*

Focusing on anything other than Jesus is sin; that includes property, money or even church. What? That's right! Many focus on their work rather than the glory of Christ. Why are you working in the church; for God's glory or yours? Please, don't get me wrong. We need more workers in the church. But, when your work becomes focused on your work it is "an empty vessel." It is possible to get so busy in church you miss Jesus.

So, I hope you understand; this is not a book about angels, it is a book about Jesus. It is about a Savior who loves us so much that he gave his life so that we can have eternal life. He has put eternal beings at our disposal, angels, so the Gospel will go to every nation. Pray about how you will be able to be the most effective and then do it.

Chapter Six

Innumerable Angels

He stood in awe of sights never seen before by man. The magnificence of the moment was breath taking. There was nothing common about the sights before him; nothing set by chance. Everything was perfectly ordered. No one could have dreamed of the wonders he beheld.

There, before him, was a Great Throne Room; the likes of which has never been seen. He stood speechless; breathless. He was not even sure he could take another breath. His mind was racing and he had to force his body to pass air through his lungs.

Before him was a court of angelic beings. The court was not quiet and stately; it was bustling with excitement and praises. This is a paraphrase of a partial account from John the Revelator as he had this vision in Heaven.

As he continues with the story he cites the presence of a multitude of angels. Revelation 5:11 says, "Then I looked and heard the voice of many angels, numbering thousands upon thousands, and ten thousand times ten thousand. They encircled the throne and the living creatures and the elders."

How many angels are there? Of course, no one really knows. The number "ten thousand times ten thousand" is already a huge number; 100 million to be exact. However, the number is most likely much higher.

The highest common number of the time was 10,000. That does not mean that was the highest number known, but it was the highest common number. For example, in the sixties the highest common number would probably be millions, in the eighties it would most likely have been billions; today we talk about trillions. We have bigger numbers, but our highest common number is trillions.

So, if John were writing Revelation today he would probably say he saw 10 trillion times 10 trillion. Get the idea? In other words, the angels are innumerable. God commands an all-powerful army that he doesn't even need. The truth is, he need only to speak and everything in the universe must submit to him. Nevertheless, these beings were created by him to be his messengers.

Hebrew 12:22 (KJV) - "But ye are come unto mount Sion, and unto the city of the living God, the heavenly Jerusalem, and to an innumerable company of angels . . ."

The power of God is unfathomable. There will be a day when

the Lord returns. He tells us to be ready for his eminent return. Satan and his angels will be gathered together and thrown into the abyss until the Final Day of Judgement.

You, however, have access to a much better scenario. You have the opportunity to accept Jesus as your Lord and Savior and live with him for eternity.

CHAPTER SEVEN

The Nephilim

Moses sent out twelve spies to the land of Canaan. God told Moses to have the men:

> *To tell of the fertility of the land See what the land is like and whether the people who live there are strong or weak, few or many. What kind of land do they live in? Is it good or bad? What kind of towns do they live in? Are they unwalled or fortified? How is the soil? Is it fertile or poor? Are there trees in it or not? Do your best to bring back some of the fruit of the land." (It was the season for the first ripe grapes.)(Numbers 13:18-20)*

When they returned, 10 of the 12 said that the land was full of milk and honey, "But the people who live there are powerful, and the cities are fortified and very large. We even saw descendants of Anak there (Numbers 13:28)." They said there are giants there, descendants of Anak, the tribe of the Nephilim. These are powerful men, renowned for their fierceness in battle. It is impossible to enter into the Promised Land.

The Nephilim were not fallen angels, they were giants. They were a tribe of giants.

Nephilim being "fallen angels" does not fit the context of the Scripture. The context of Scripture includes the entire Bible. People who believe the Bible contradicts itself are those who do not put the Scripture in the context of the entire Bible. Plus, they have their own agenda that they want to purport instead of the agenda of God.

Many people are more interested in winning an argument than they are of stating or recognizing the truth. The truth is the "argument" about the Nephilim is of little consequence. Even though I heard it stated on the radio just the other day that those who do not understand the Nephilim do not understand the Scripture.

NO! Those who do not understand that the focus of Scripture is Jesus do not understand the Bible. God's Word points to Jesus in every way, because he is the salvation of the world. Neither angels, nor the Nephilim nor the principalities and powers are the focus in the Bible. Christ is THE focus of the Word of God.

Now that we have settled that, we can study about the Nephilim, but it will most likely not feed your craving for mysticism. Even though I believe that Scripture proves that the Nephilim were not fallen angels, I included them in this book because so many believe they are. It is important to learn the truth about the entire Word of God; not choosing Scriptures for your own agenda.

Genesis 6:4 says, "There were giants in the earth in those days; and also after that, when the sons of God came in unto the daughters of men, and they bare children to them, the same became mighty men which were of old, men of renown."

When studying the Bible, it is best to let the Bible exegete itself; (Exegete is a fancy word for explain or expound upon.) this verse exegetes itself. Let's start in the Hebrew. The Hebrew is the original language that the Old Testament was given to the writers. Therefore, it is important to go back to the original text to be able to understand it.

The Hebrew word for "giants" is "nĕphiyl" which is where we get the word "Nephilim." However the translation for the word "nĕphiyl" is "giants" not "angels." Furthermore, if one continues within the context of the Scripture, one can learn that the "nĕphiyl" were a tribe of people.

Numbers 13:33 says that the "Nephilim" came from the tribe of Anak. God has always called men the "sons of God." If you are well versed in the Bible you might possibly be saying, "Wait a minute Rick, the Bible calls angels the sons of God in the book of Job. Let's examine that Scripture.

Job 1:6 says, "Now there was a day when the sons of God came to present themselves before the LORD, and Satan came also among them."

Job 2:1 says, "Again there was a day when the sons of God came to present themselves before the LORD, and Satan came also among them to present himself before the LORD." In the book of Job the term "sons of God" is used as familiarity. In other words, this is to show that those who were before God were spirits as well. The stood in the Throne room of God. Job is the only book in the Bible that places "sons of God" outside the physicality of man. Therefore, the context of the Scripture, the entire Bible, places the context of Job as familiarity and the context of Genesis with mankind.

In other words, the sons of God in Genesis were men. How can I state that? Very simply; again the passage exegetes (explains) itself. Continue with me in Genesis 6:4. It says, ". . . when the sons of God came in unto the daughters of men, and they bare children to them, the same became mighty men which were of old, men of renown." Mighty men! Not man/gods, not man/angels, but mighty MEN! Plus, one has to also consider the Scripture in Numbers 13 that says the Nephilim were a tribe of giant people.

Why would that not dispel the argument on the Nephilim, perhaps because it's not as exciting; I don't know. Nevertheless, the Bible states the explanation rather plainly.

Still not convinced? The Hebrew word for "son" is "ben." "Ben" not only means "son," but according Strong's concordance, it also means "A member of a guild, order, class." This would place the correct translation in the book of Job as possibly saying, ""Now there was a day when the *order* of God came to present themselves before the LORD, and Satan came also among them"; the order of God being spiritual beings.

Some say the "sons of God" in Genesis are fallen angels. It reads, ". . . the same became mighty men which were of old, men of renown." However, as was previously stated it says, "Men" of renown. Not demons, not angelic, but men.

In the book of Mark chapter 12 the Sadducees came to Jesus to ask him a question. They were trying to "trip him up" and trap him into denying the Scripture. Mark 12:18-23 says:

> *Then the Sadducees, who say there is no resurrection, came to him with a question. "Teacher," they said, "Moses wrote for us that if a man's brother dies and leaves a wife but no children, the man must marry the widow and raise up offspring for his brother. Now there were seven brothers. The first one married and died without leaving any children. The second one married the widow, but he also died, leaving no child. It was the same with the third. In fact, none of the seven left any children. Last of all, the woman died too. At the resurrection whose wife will she be, since the seven were married to her?"*

The answer Jesus gave answers the question of the Nephilim. He says in Mark 12:24-25:

> *Jesus replied, "Are you not in error because you do not know the Scriptures or the power of God? When the dead rise, they will neither marry nor be given in marriage; they will be like the angels in heaven.*

In other words, they do not procreate because they are

neither male no female. Therefore, angels could not mate with humans. Angels are created beings, but not like God made man. Man was commanded to multiply and fill the earth (Genesis 1:28).

No matter whether one is studying angels or other Scriptures in the Bible, one must put the entire Bible into context. It is not expedient to study the Bible in the light of fads. Going back to the original text helps one have a better understanding of the Scripture. Do not read into the Scripture what is not there, but exegete the passage from the context of the entire Word of God.

Chapter Eight

Demons vs. Angels

He plotted with his followers to overthrow the Power that ruled the universe. He made the case to those who would listen, "If you will follow me we will be great and rule the universe. We no longer need anyone to tell us what to do. We are powerful and do not need God!"

This was most likely a scene in heaven before Satan was cast out with one third of God's angels following him. Isn't that what Mankind has done on this earth. Every type and form of religion has been devised so that man can "rule himself." The folly of that thinking is immeasurable. Can a man plan what happens the day after his death? Of course not! Like Satan and his angels, man has been trying to be in control since the Garden of Eden.

Just like he tricked his angels in following him, Satan came to Eve with the promise of greatness. Genesis 3:6 says, "When the woman saw that the fruit of the tree was good for food and pleasing to the eye, and also desirable for gaining wisdom, she took some and ate it. She also gave some to her husband, who was with her, and he ate it." Notice it says, ". . . also desirable for gaining wisdom." What wisdom was she looking for? The wisdom of God! The previous verse has the serpent, Satan, saying, "For God knows that when you eat from it your eyes will be opened, and you will be like God, knowing good and evil." She was looking to be like God.

Man has been doing the same thing ever since. 1 Corinthians 11:3 says, "But I am afraid that just as Eve was deceived by the serpent's cunning, your minds may somehow be led astray from your sincere and pure devotion to Christ." Satan still works from the same playbook in the twenty-first Century! Because of the arrogance of man, he does not need to change his tactic. If something works why change it?

- Barak Obama, "We are no longer a Christian Nation"

- Oprah Winfrey, "There are many ways to get to heaven outside of Jesus"

- Rick Warren, "Rick Warren, Bill Hybels, megachurch pastors, speakers: Christians and Muslims should build relationships which 'genuinely reflect our common love for God and for one another'."

- Joel Osteen in an interview with Larry King, "Answering whether Jews or Muslims would go to heaven, he was noncommittal, 'You know, I'm very careful about saying who would and wouldn't go to heaven... I spent a lot of time in India with my father. I don't know all about their religion. But I know they love God. And I don't know. I've seen their sincerity. So I don't know'."

Translation of all of these comments: The Bible is not true. Anyone can go to heaven if they sincerely love God. However, one has to ask, "Which God?" You might be thinking, "Rick, if there is one God of the universe wouldn't that mean that everyone is worshipping him?" It is true that there is only on true God, he is Yahweh. He is the Creator of the universe. He makes up the Triune Godhead of the Father, Jesus, the Son and the Holy Spirit. Even so, many worship the gods they have created themselves. Allah, Buddha, Hindu gods and goddesses and even those who claim to worship Jesus but worship him in their own image instead of the image of God are not worshipping the one True God.

God has told us in his Word how we are to approach a Holy God. There is only one way, that way is through Jesus. John 3:36 says, "Whoever believes in the Son has eternal life, but whoever rejects the Son will not see life, for God's wrath remains on them."

1 John 5:10 says:

Whoever believes in the Son of God accepts this testimony. Whoever does not believe God has made him out to be a liar, because they have not believed the testimony God has given about his Son. And this is the testimony: God has given us eternal life, and this life is in his Son. Whoever

61

has the Son has life; whoever does not have the Son of God does not have life.

2 John 1:9 says:

Anyone who runs ahead and does not continue in the teaching of Christ does not have God; whoever continues in the teaching has both the Father and the Son. If anyone comes to you and does not bring this teaching, do not take them into your house or welcome them. Anyone who welcomes them shares in their wicked work."

Can it get any more plain than the above Scriptures? The last part of the last Scripture above really states the point. Does Islam, Buddhism, Hinduism, Mormonism, or any other "ism" teach that Jesus is the only Way, the Truth and The Life? No! Each one says that you must have something other than Jesus to spend eternal life in heaven.

This was the lie that Satan began the fall with and coaxed his demonic followers to believe. Before the fall, they were all considered angels; after the fall, the fall of Satan, they were called demons.

Demons and Angels are essentially the same type of spirit being. However, the fallen angels that followed Satan are now called Demons. The angels that represent God are his holy angels.

The demons who were cast out of heaven, like Lucifer, knew

first hand of the greatness of God. Nevertheless, they decided that they could be better than God and his angels. Therefore, as is described in Isaiah 14:13-15:

You said in your heart, "I will ascend to the heavens; I will raise my throne above the stars of God; I will sit enthroned on the mount of assembly, on the utmost heights of Mount Zaphon. I will ascend above the tops of the clouds; I will make myself like the Most High." But you are brought down to the realm of the dead, to the depths of the pit."

Ezekiel 28:13-17 says:

You were in Eden, the garden of God; every precious stone adorned you: carnelian, chrysolite and emerald, topaz, onyx and jasper, lapis lazuli, turquoise and beryl. Your settings and mountings were made of gold; on the day you were created they were prepared. You were anointed as a guardian cherub, for so I ordained you.

You were on the holy mount of God; you walked among the fiery stones. You were blameless in your ways from the day you were created till wickedness was found in you. Through your widespread trade you were filled with violence, and you sinned.

So I drove you in disgrace from the mount of God, and I expelled you, guardian cherub, from among the fiery stones. Your heart became proud on account of your beauty, and you corrupted your wisdom because of your splendor.

So I threw you to the earth; I made a spectacle of you before kings.

Lucifer and Satan are one in the same. Lucifer is translated in the King James Version and means: "light-bearer, shining one, morning star, Lucifer of the king of Babylon and Satan (Strong's Concordance). Satan was thrown from heaven because of his pride; he thought he could be God! The angels who followed Lucifer did not choose wisely. Because of his appearance they thought he was the most powerful, but he was only the deceiver.

Rev 12:3-9 says:

Then another sign appeared in heaven: an enormous red dragon with seven heads and ten horns and seven crowns on its heads. Its tail swept a third of the stars out of the sky and flung them to the earth . . . Then war broke out in heaven. Michael and his angels fought against the dragon, and the dragon and his angels fought back. But he was not strong enough, and they lost their place in heaven. The great dragon was hurled down—that ancient serpent called the devil, or Satan, who leads the whole world astray. He was hurled to the earth, and his angels with him.

We know that hell was prepared for the devil and his angels, according to Matthew 25:41: "Then He will say to those on His left, 'Depart from me, you who are cursed, into the eternal fire prepared for the devil and his angels'." Some of the demons are bound in the abyss until which time as they are unleashed onto the earth as a judgment from God because of the rebellion of man.

It is evident from the Scriptures that Angels of God are more powerful than the demons. Why? Because the angels of God are backed up by his power. God does not need his angels to protect him because he is an aging old man sitting on a throne. No! He is the Creator of the universe and at any second, if he so desired, could wipe out the entire universe including angels and demons and start over. But that is not his plan.

God is a relational God. He created his creation to share the majesty of his universe for eternity. But because of the freewill of man and angels, men and spirit alike get to choose where they will spend eternity.

God does not send anyone to Hell. Even Satan and his angels chose where they would spend eternity. God gives every individual the power to choose. One can choose to live with God in heaven or choose to live where God is not; that place is called Hell. He has also prescribed the way to accept his offer to live with him; that is through is only begotten Son, Jesus Christ.

Oprah said, "Surely there must be other ways to come to God. If he is so magnificent, there must be many ways to reach him." The folly of that statement is seen in the following example:

> Washington (CNN) -- Two people without invitations crashed President Obama's first

White House state dinner, the U.S. Secret Service said Wednesday. The Secret Service confirmed a Washington Post report that the couple who crashed Tuesday night's dinner were Tareq and Michaele Salahi. . . . The couple's names did not appear on the guest list distributed Tuesday by the White House. . . . Lying to the Secret Service could bring a felony charge, Townsend said. (http://www.cnn.com/2009/POLITICS/11/25/state.dinner.crashers/index.html)

What's the big deal? The Whitehouse is huge and the President of the United States is the most powerful man in the world. These people did no harm so why were they detained? Because President Obama had a specific way to come to the Whitehouse; by invitation only. One cannot go to Washington and simply stroll into the Oval Office. One must be invited.

How much more a Holy God? How much more secure does God want his heaven to be? God will not allow a Satan worshipper or a worshiper of any other God in his heaven. Those worshipers must go where there god will be for eternity and that is the place that has been prepared separate from God; a place called Hell.

So, are there differences between demons of Satan and angels of God? Absolutely! The difference is that the angels of God submit to the Creator of the universe. The angels of Satan, the demons, submit to the creator of deception, Satan.

Chapter Nine

Can Satan Read Minds?

Solomon was not the perfect leader; he was not even the kindest leader. 1 Kings 12 depicts Solomon as more of a tyrant than a kind and benevolent king. Nevertheless, Israel was blessed under him. Why? Because he honored God.

1Kings 8:22 says:

> *Then Solomon stood before the altar of the Lord in front of the whole assembly of Israel, spread out his hands toward heaven and said: Lord, the God of Israel, there is no God like you in heaven above or on earth below – you who keep your covenant of love with your servants who continue wholeheartedly in your way."*

Solomon, with all of his faults honored God. At the time of writing this book we are closing in on the end of a very difficult presidential campaign. Even so, there is no president that can fix the situation America is in.

There is only one hope; that is for whoever is president to stand before the entire United States of America, raise his hands and proclaim that we are a Christian nation who worships God the Father, God the Son and God the Holy Spirit. That is the only hope our nation has to survive. Without God – Yahweh, we are doomed to destruction.

Satan can hear the rhetoric that is spewed from both candidates; he is not afraid. Neither candidate is calling on God. Both are declaring that they have the answer for our existing problems. The truth is, without God, neither has the answer.

Can Satan read our thoughts? The short answer to that question is, "No!" But there are things the Christian should understand to help him or her win the battle.

Satan is neither omnipresent (everywhere at the same time) nor omniscient (all-knowing) nor is he omnipotent (all-powerful). He is a supernatural being, but has many of the same limitations we have.

If you are under attack, it is most likely not Satan who is leading the fight. He has given orders to his minions to attack those who oppose him, much the same way a General would give to those in his command in a war.

Demons have to report back to Satan for him to be able to make a decision on your behalf and, more than likely, the subordinates make the decisions for the small skirmish the demon is in charge of.

Satan is also limited by the knowledge or intelligence he can compile on you. That is one of the main reasons that it is not good to speak negative. Satan can use your words against you, but only if he knows your words.

In other words, when you speak your fears, he knows how to attack. He cannot read your mind. Only God knows the thoughts of man.

1 Kings 8:39 says, ". . . Forgive and act; deal with everyone according to all they do, since you know their hearts (for you alone know every human heart) . . ." There is no one else who has that ability. God knows what we will say before we can say it, while the thought is still formulating (Psalm 139:4). Jesus, being God incarnate, exhibited the divine quality of knowing men's thoughts: "He knew what was in each person" (John 2:25; cf. Matthew 9:4; John 6:64).

God knows your prayers before you pray them. Satan does not have that ability. Maybe you are thinking, "Should I pray out loud? Satan will know what I am praying." Yes that is true, but the power of God that resides within you is greater than Satan. When you pray in the will of God you will be victorious. However, when you speak negative, which is against the will of God, you give Satan and his demons a foot hold against you.

Repent! Allow God to fight the battle for you. Don't give the enemy any weapons to fight against you. When you speak, speak the word. Ephesians 4:29 says, "Do not let any unwholesome talk come out of your mouths, but only what is helpful for building others up according to their needs, that it may benefit those who listen."

We are all imperfect. So, I have been around very positive people in my life, and without exception there are times when they speak negative. So, it is important to keep a relationship with the Father and repent of unwholesome talk. Ask forgiveness and then move on; keeping in mind that there may be consequences for the words you have spoken.

CHAPTER TEN

What Do Angels Look Like?

Angels are fearsome creatures; powerful and daunting. Many times when they appear they first say, "Fear Not!" Then, they begin the message. Angels are not little cupids with wings or frail figures; they are powerful warriors.

In the armed services, messengers are those who have to go behind enemy lines to deliver messages vital to winning the battle. They are trained to elude or encounter the enemy if needed. Angels are messengers for God, willing and able to take the battle to the enemy if necessary to deliver the message God has for the recipient.

The guards of Jesus' tomb became as dead men when they saw the angel of the Lord (Matthew 28:4). The shepherds in the fields in Luke 2 were "sore afraid" when the angel of the Lord appeared and the glory of the Lord shone around them.

The Angels have been in the very presence of God. Every time Moses went up on the mountain to meet with God he had to wear a veil; the glory of the Lord was too bright for the people to behold. The Angels are with God day and night, so it is not their own glory that makes them bright in appearance, it is the glory of the Lord. The Book of Revelation says that there will be no need for the sun in God's Kingdom because he will be the Light for the ages.

Angels seem to have many appearances. As we will discuss later, some angels appear as humans. Some angels appear in the glory of the Lord such as those who brought the news of the arrival of Jesus to the shepherds in Luke chapter two.

There are only four angels named in the Bible; two are fallen angels and two serve God.

- Abaddon, Apollyon - Abaddon is the Angel of the bottomless pit who appears to be a ruler of evil spirits as described in the book of Revelation. The word Abaddon used in the Old Testament is a place of destruction. (Psalm 88:11; Proverbs 15:11; 27:20).

- Rev. 9:11, "They have as king over them, the angel of the abyss; his name in Hebrew is Abaddon, and in the Greek he has the name Apollyon."

Gabriel means "warrior of God" or "man of God" an archangel; the angel God used to send messages of great importance to man; sent to Daniel, to Zacharias, and to Mary (Strong's)." He appears to be one who carries messages. He is an Archangel who appeared to Daniel as a man and gave him the meaning of a vision. In the New Testament he appeared to Zechariah who was serving in the temple in order to announce the birth of John the Baptist. Six months later he appeared to Mary, informing her that she would be the mother of Jesus.

- Daniel 8:16, "And I heard the voice of a man between the banks of Ulai, and he called out and said, "Gabriel, give this man an understanding of the vision."

- Daniel 9:21, "while I was still speaking in prayer, then the man Gabriel, whom I had seen in the vision previously, came to me in my extreme weariness about the time of the evening offering."

- Luke 1:19, "The angel answered and said to him, 'I am Gabriel, who stands in the presence of God, and I have been sent to speak to you and to bring you this good news'."

- Luke 1:26, "Now in the sixth month the angel Gabriel was sent from God to a city in Galilee called Nazareth."

Michael means: "Who is like God, one of the chief, or the first, archangel who is described as the one who stands in time of conflict for the children of Israel (Strong's)."

- Daniel 10:13, "But the prince of the kingdom of Persia was withstanding me for twenty-one days; then behold, Michael, one of the chief princes, came to help me, for I had been left there with the kings of Persia."

- Daniel 12:1, "Now at that time Michael, the great prince who stands guard over the sons of your people, will arise. And there will be a time of distress such as never occurred since there was a nation until that time; and at that time your people, everyone who is found written in the book, will be rescued."

- Jude 9, "But Michael the archangel, when he disputed with the devil and argued about the body of Moses, did not dare pronounce against him a railing judgment, but said, "The Lord rebuke you!"

- Revelation 12:7-8, "And there was war in heaven, Michael and his angels waging war with the dragon. The dragon and his angels waged war, and they (angels of Satan) were not strong enough, and there was no longer a place found for them in heaven (Parenthesis added)."

Satan means: "adversary, one who withstands, superhuman adversary (Strong's). Satan is the adversary of God and mankind. He is the fallen angel, the devil, who rebelled against God. He's mentioned many times in the Old and New Testaments. He has many names in the Bible such as Lucifer, Adversary, Dark One, etc. Satan looks many different ways and comes in many forms. He rarely appears as a creature with horns and a tail. 2 Corinthians 11:14 says, ". . . Satan himself masquerades as an angel of light."

- Matt 4:10, "Then Jesus said to him, 'Go, Satan! For it is written, 'You shall worship the Lord your God, and serve Him only'.'"

- Mark 1:13, "And He (Jesus) was in the wilderness forty days being tempted by Satan; and He was with the wild beasts, and the angels were ministering to Him."

- Luke 22:3, "And Satan entered into Judas who was called Iscariot, belonging to the number of the twelve."

- Rom. 16:20, "The God of peace will soon crush Satan under your feet. The grace of our Lord Jesus be with you."

- 2 Cor. 11:14, "No wonder, for even Satan disguises himself as an angel of light."

- Rev. 12:9, "And the great dragon was thrown down, the serpent of old who is called the devil and Satan, who deceives the whole world; he was thrown down to the earth, and his angels were thrown down with him."

Cherubim - Ezekiel 10:20 – "This is the living creature that I saw under the God of Israel by the river of Chebar; and I knew that they were the cherubims. Every one had four faces apiece, and every one four wings; and the likeness of the hands of a man was under their wings. And the likeness of their faces was the same faces which I saw by the river of Chebar, their appearances and themselves: they went every one straight forward."

- Chebar means, "far-off"; a Babylonian river near which many Israelite exiles settled; maybe the 'Habor' or the 'Royal Canal' of Nebuchadnezzar

Archangels means "chief of the angels" - The Jews, after the exile, distinguished several orders of angels; some reckoned four angels (according to the four sides of God's throne) of the highest rank; but the majority reckoned seven (after the pattern of the seven Amshaspands, the highest spirits of the religion of Zoroaster) (Strong's).

- 1 Thessalonians 4:16 - For the Lord himself will come down from heaven, with a loud command, with the voice of the archangel and with the trumpet call of God, and the dead in Christ will rise first.

- Jude 1:9 - But even the archangel Michael, when he was disputing with the devil about the body of Moses, did not himself dare to condemn him for slander but said, "The Lord rebuke you!"

- Seraphim – "Seraph, majestic beings with 6 wings, human hands or voices in attendance upon God.

- Isaiah 6:2 - Above him were seraphim, each with six wings: With two wings they covered their faces, with two they covered their feet, and with two they were flying. Majestic beings with 6 wings, human hands or voices in attendance upon God.

- Isaiah 6:6 - Then one of the seraphim flew to me with a live coal in his hand, which he had taken with tongs from the altar.

It can be said that Angels are fierce looking creatures that are strong warriors for God. They are not wimpy looking little cupids with tiny wings, neither are they feminine looking. Every instance of angels in the Bible is a figure in the appearance of a male. That is not to say they are males. Jesus said they are neither male nor female.

CHAPTER ELEVEN

Guardian Angels

God has made promises to his people, if those chosen by God will obey him, they will be blessed. I am not a "name it and claim it" preacher. Nevertheless, I do believe that God keeps his word and blesses those who are obedient to him. The obedience begins with accepting his Son. Even so, that is not where it ends. It is possible to know Jesus and yet not be fully obedient to God.

Has God ever impressed on you to do something that you didn't listen to? Do you give God your money according to what he has placed in your heart to give? Have you ever gone over the speed limit? See, Christians know that they are not perfect but, if they have accepted Christ, they are still saved. But, there are blessings you are giving up if you are not obedient to God's Word.

God gave Israel certain promises if they are obedient. Those same promises are in affect today. It does not have anything to do with salvation; it has to do with obedience. However, there is only one act of obedience to be saved. John 6:28-29 says, "Then they asked him, 'What must we do to do the works God requires?' Jesus answered, 'The work of God is this: to believe in the one he has sent'." After that one form of obedience one will be accepted by the Father on his terms for eternal salvation. But it is not where it ends. God told Moses at Mt. Sinai to tell Israel about his promises. Exodus 23:20-25 says:

"See, I am sending an angel ahead of you to guard you along the way and to bring you to the place I have prepared. Pay attention to him and listen to what he says. Do not rebel against him; he will not forgive your rebellion, since my Name is in him. If you listen carefully to what he says and do all that I say, I will be an enemy to your enemies and will oppose those who oppose you. My angel will go ahead of you and bring you into the land of the Amorites, Hittites, Perizzites, Canaanites, Hivites and Jebusites, and I will wipe them out. Do not bow down before their gods or worship them or follow their practices. You must demolish them and break their sacred stones to pieces. Worship the LORD your God, and his blessing will be on your food and water. I will take away sickness from among you . . ."

We have the promises of God today. If you trust in God, he sends angels before you to prepare the way. The best thing is Jesus camps around you. Psalm 34:7 says, "The angel of the LORD encamps around those who fear him, and he delivers them." In this case, the angel of the Lord has to be Jesus. Why? Because, even though angels are feared creatures, for those who know God they are not to be feared. Matthew 10:28 says,

"Do not be afraid of those who kill the body but cannot kill the soul. Rather, be afraid of the One who can destroy both soul and body in hell." Psalm 34 is very clear that this angel should be feared. Plus, angels are not omnipresent (everywhere at the same time). The angel of Psalm 34 "encamps around those who fear him." He is all around those he protects.

Angels are fierce. An angel killed 185,000 Assyrians. Isaiah 37:36 says, "Then the angel of the LORD went out and put to death a hundred and eighty-five thousand in the Assyrian camp. When the people got up the next morning—there were all the dead bodies!" One angel killed 185,000. Yet Jesus encamps around those who fear him.

Why is Jesus to be feared? For the Christian, it is not the kind of fear the world understands. Christ must be respected and loved. He is feared for the authority he has. Even so, for those who call on his name, he is the Protector. John 1:12 says, "Yet to all who did receive him, to those who believed in his name, he gave the right to become children of God—children born not of natural descent, nor of human decision or a husband's will, but born of God."

Therefore, Christians fear God out of respect because we are his children. Non-believers must fear God because he has the power to condemn them to hell if they reject him.

So, it can be said that we are not only protected by Jesus, but he will pursue anyone seeking to do harm to the Christian. Psalm 35:5 – "May they be like chaff before the wind, with the angel of the LORD driving them away; may their path be dark and slippery, with the angel of the LORD pursuing them."

Where do guardian angels come into the equation? The guardian angels are fighting the war against the demons. In fact, those who do not know Christ have a guardian angel assigned to them to keep Satan from destroying them before they have had the chance to accept Christ.

Angels also come to unsuspecting people and Christians as a test and/or learning experience to show the power of God. These types of angels are most likely guardians. As stated earlier Hebrews 13:2 says, "Be not forgetful to entertain strangers: for thereby some have entertained angels unawares."

There are not many angels mentioned in the New Testament. Possibly it is because we walk in the power of the Holy Spirit and Satan cannot harm you. The Bible says that we have the power to resist the devil and he must flee; that includes his demons. The absence of the angels in the New Testament is proof of the power of God in you. That is not to say that angels are no longer here for us; they most assuredly are. The battle still rages. But it is to say that we walk in the power of God to send Satan away.

Jesus said, "Greater things than these will you do in my name (John 14:12)." It is also interesting that angels reappear in power in the book of Revelation; possibly, because miracles will increase during the last days of Revelation.

Obviously, there are angels in the New Testament but, for the most part, they were before the resurrection of Jesus and before he sent the Comforter; the Holy Spirit. The angels that were at the tomb were messengers to proclaim the resurrection of Jesus.

I think it is important to point out that, as a Christian, you must prepare. You must be diligent. Do not follow what the world says, follow the word.

The absolute pre- Rapture theology you have heard of is not in the Bible. There are some who have interpreted the pre-tribulation Rapture into the Bible. But it is not plain. Prophecy is never totally understood until it comes to fruition. At that point we stand back and say, "Oh, so that's what it meant. " Be prepared!

Be prepared for a way that may not have been explained by the theologian. What if the Pre-Tribulation is wrong? Are you going to take the Mark because it is not supposed to happen until after the rapture? God forbid! Stop looking for the Rapture. Look to Jesus. Follow Jesus! It is he that we must look to for our guide.

Forget about the Rapture, follow Christ. Prepare for persecution. Prepare to stand strong for Christ no matter the circumstance.

It is not angels that we trust in; it is Jesus. Don't trust the angel to save you; trust God.

CHAPTER TWELVE

The Last Days

It is time for the Elect to prepare for the return of the Lord Jesus. 2 Peter 3:3-13 says:

> *But the day of the Lord will come like a thief. The heavens will disappear with a roar; the elements will be destroyed by fire, and the earth and everything done in it will be laid bare. Since everything will be destroyed in this way, what kind of people ought you to be? You ought to live holy and godly lives as you look forward to the day of God and speed its coming. That day will bring about the destruction of the heavens by fire, and the elements will melt in the heat. But in keeping with his promise we are looking forward to a new heaven and a new earth, where righteousness dwells.*

The Church, in its quest to be "relevant," has lost its relevancy. The world is craving the truth. Unfortunately, the Church, because of its lack of power and discernment, believes that the world wants Hollywood or Broadway with a spiritual flavor. The "Church" believes that if it is enough like the world, the world will want to be a part of it. The folly of this thinking came from Jesus himself. He said, "If you belonged to the world, it would love you as its own. As it is, you do not belong to the world, but I have chosen you out of the world. That is why the world hates you."

The real problem lies in the fact that the world does not hate the Church, because she is not speaking the truth. She is tickling the ears of sinners. 2 Timothy 4:3 says, "For the time will come when they will not endure sound doctrine; but after their own lusts shall they heap to themselves teachers, having itching ears . . ."

Rick Warren believes we should practice Chrislam, a mixture of Christianity and Islam; Hillsong Church just had a Broadway style show including The Naked Cowboy impersonator in his underwear and a bearded man as Lady Liberty. Where has the Church gone?

The SBC (Southern Baptist Convention) has just filed a petition to the court to aid in the building of a mosque in New Jersey, even though the people were against it.

- June 15, 2016 - The Ethics & Religious Liberty Commission received criticism from some members of the Southern Baptist Convention at the denomination's annual meeting on Wednesday for filing an amicus brief on behalf of a Muslim group seeking to build a mosque.

In May, the ERLC joined a diverse coalition of groups in an amicus brief to support the Islamic Society of Basking Ridge in its lawsuit against a New Jersey township that rejected its application to build a mosque. (Southern Baptist Convention on Wednesday, St, Louis, Missouri, on June 15, 2016. Read more at http://www.christianpost.com/news/erlcs-russell-moore-takes-heat-sbc-supporting-religious-freedom-muslims-build-mosque-165299/#98BE3AwSmZ1m3Bto.99)

- An amicus curiae (amicus brief) is a 'friend of the court', a person who is not actually involved in a case as a party but who brings a matter to the attention of the court. Usually the issue involves the public interest. It is not a universally applicable procedure (Collins Dictionary of Law © W.J. Stewart, 2006).

Judges 6:25 says, "That same night the LORD said to him, 'Take the second bull from your father's herd, the one seven years old. Tear down your father's altar to Baal and cut down the Asherah pole beside it'."

I wonder if God wants us to do different today. I wonder if now we are to build altars to Baal. Contrary to what the politically correct might have said, Muslims do not worship the same god as we do. 1 John 5:12 says, "Whoever has the Son has life; whoever does not have the Son of God does not have life." John 5:22-29 says:

Moreover, the Father judges no one, but has entrusted all judgment to the Son, that all may honor the Son just as they honor the Father. Whoever does not honor the Son does not honor the Father, who sent him. "Very truly I tell you, whoever hears my word and believes him who sent me has eternal life and will not be judged but has crossed over from death to life . . ."

1 John 2:23 says, "No one who denies the Son has the Father; whoever acknowledges the Son has the Father also." Muslims deny the Son. Israel denies the Son as well. Even though I believe Israel prays to Yahweh, the Father of creation, the same God as we do, I do not believe they get a pass. If they do not accept Jesus, they will be condemned as well. I would not advocate building a synagogue either. Nevertheless, God has given a special promise to Abraham that the Jewish nation will come to him. That being said, the Jews have rejected Christ so far and will be judged as well.

A huge difference for me is in the fact that Muslims worship the moon god, a form of Baal worship. The Jews worship Yahweh, the Creator of the universe. Even though the Jews have not accepted Christ yet, I believe there will be a time that they will recognize that Jesus was the Messiah and they missed him; then they will repent and be saved.

I have to make it clear that we are to give the Gospel to the Muslims, the Jews and any other person who does not know Christ. That does not mean that I want to help a Satanist build a temple to Satan the name of loving your neighbor.

The Bible says that we are to be wise as serpents and harmless as doves (Matthew 10:26). Building the temple of Baal does not seem like wisdom.

When you look at many of the pictures of Baal, the symbol is a moon with a star; just like that of Islam. Daniel did not support the worship of Nebucudnezzar in the name of religious freedom. He was not worried that he would not be able to worship if he did not "go along" as the ERLC of SBC.

The Pope has decided we should embrace Islam as well. The Voice of Russia Radio, June 21, 2016 said:

> During his visit last week to Jordan Israel, and the Palestinian Authority, Pope Francis invited Israeli President Shimon Peres and Palestinian Authority President Mahmoud Abbas.
>
> Peres's spokesperson has announced in Times of Israel that Abbas, Peres, and Pope Francis will be joined by Jewish, Christian and Islamic religious leaders.
>
> According to the officials, these evening prayers would be a "pause in politics" and have no political aim behind it other than the desire to bring peace and respect to the Israeli-Palestinian relations, states the Associated Press.

The Vatican will broadcast the event worldwide through the official website.

> However, Rev. Pierbattista Pizzaballa, the custodian of Catholic Church property in the

Holy Land has announced that people should keep their expectations low when it comes to this event.

[No-one should think] "peace will suddenly break out on Monday, or that peace is any closer," he said to AP.

The Vatican has also announced that on Friday, the Pope also held a meeting with Japanese Prime Minister Shinzo Abe, and both leaders discussed possible ways of promoting peace and stability in Asia.

Read more: http://sputniknews.com/voiceofrussia/ news/2014_06_07/Vatican-to-hold-Islamic-prayers- for-the-first-time-in-history-9001/

Why would God change his commandment, "You shall have no other gods before me"?

I was listening to Rick Wiles on Trunews recently. He had been invited to a pastor conference with the pastoral "leaders" of the country. I listened with mixed emotion as he gave his report. Sadly, my mixed feelings came from the reaction of the pastors; not Trump.

Rick said that Trump answered the question honestly and was forth coming with the plan to give the power back to the church. He said he was going to do away with the rule about 501(c)3.

For those who do not know, when Senator Lyndon Baines Johnson proposed a 501(c) prohibition program barring pastors from supporting a candidate from the pulpit. In essence he did two things with "one fell swoop." He denied the Constitution on the separation of church and state and freedom of speech at the same time. Furthermore, the word "prohibition" should have given the pastors of the time a clue as to the intent of the proposition. Nevertheless, pastors around the country "caved in" to the pressures from the legislation. The same thing continues today, and Christians sit idly by while the government, who is supposed to be "We the People," oversteps its boundaries and takes away liberty.

My sadness comes from those pastors who did not challenge the original prohibition and even more for those who walk in fear. How can one call himself a leader if he walks in fear? Satan is the god of fear; 2 Timothy 2:14 says, "For the Spirit God gave us does not make us timid, but gives us power, love and self-discipline."

The Internal Revenue Service website elaborates upon this prohibition as follows:

> Under the Internal Revenue Code, all section 501(c)(3) organizations are absolutely prohibited from directly or indirectly participating in, or intervening in, any political campaign on behalf of (or in opposition to) any candidate for elective public office. Contributions to political campaign funds or public statements of position (verbal

or written) made on behalf of the organization in favor of or in opposition to any candidate for public office clearly violate the prohibition against political campaign activity. Violating this prohibition may result in denial or revocation of tax-exempt status and the imposition of certain excise taxes.

Certain activities or expenditures may not be prohibited depending on the facts and circumstances. For example, certain voter education activities (including presenting public forums and publishing voter education guides) conducted in a non-partisan manner do not constitute prohibited political campaign activity. In addition, other activities intended to encourage people to participate in the electoral process, such as voter registration and get-out-the-vote drives, would not be prohibited political campaign activity if conducted in a non-partisan manner.

On the other hand, voter education or registration activities with evidence of bias that (a) would favor one candidate over another; (b) oppose a candidate in some manner; or (c) have the effect of favoring a candidate or group of candidates, will constitute prohibited participation or intervention.

The Internal Revenue Service provides resources to exempt organizations and the public to help them understand the prohibition. As part of its examination program, the IRS also monitors whether organizations are complying with the prohibition.

Ironically, if the church would get up and check the law, it would find out that churches are exempt from the 501(c)3 prohibition. Yep, that's right! I know it might as a shock to believe the U.S. government would lie, but the church has been lied to by the IRS and the IRS knows that they are not required to adhere to the prohibition. Nevertheless, churches lack the fortitude to stand up against the government for any reason.

Back to Rick's Washington experience with Trump. As Mr. Trump continued to talk, he said that he perceived "fear" from the pastors he talked with. FEAR! (That was my response not Trumps.) Why would pastors have fear? Trump was told by many pastor they were afraid of losing their 501(c)3 status. But it goes much deeper than that.

The Church has lost the power of the Holy Spirit, because it has relied on the "power" of the government. Today churches believe in "Government We Trust!" God has been successfully removed from every aspect of the American culture including the church. A pastor has no business walking in fear.

I want to make it clear; I am not all high and mighty. I do

experience fear, but I trust God and walk in the power of the Holy Spirit. Experiencing fear and walking in fear is two very different things.

When the world says the Church must stop, pastors should be saying, "Move forward!" If the Church continues to conform to the world without repentance, God will judge the Church and the world.

If the church is waiting for the government, Donald Trump, Hillary Clinton or anything other than Jesus to save it, she is doomed already. It is evident in the compromise I am witnessing in the SBC, the Vatican and Mega church pastors, as well as, many small town pastors, the church leadership must come to God and repent. Then, the pastor must take up the Cross and proclaim to the world that the Church will stand for Jesus. This "namby-pamby" attitude of the church is not glorifying to God; it is an abomination to him.

The angels are here to support the Church in these last days; but more than that, we have the power of the Holy Spirit to walk in power. Salvation is not about the angels, it is about Jesus Christ.

It is not necessary for one to see the angels to have courage. The courage of God resides in every believer if he or she will allow the Holy Spirit to work. God has given gifts to every believer, but the believer must be willing to use the gift or gifts he or she has been given.

Maybe you are asking, "How do I use my gift? Pray for the sick, step out and give the Gospel. Listen to God and proclaim what he has told you to say. Step up and be bold.

It is time for the Church to understand that we can no longer conform to the world. We must proclaim the Gospel in his power. We cannot continue to follow the "leaders" of the American church if they are not going to operate in the power of the Holy Spirit. When the "leaders" succumb to chrislam, naked cowboys in the church and building temples to Baal the Church of Jesus Christ must stand for Jesus.

God has sent his angels as a support for the Church. More than that, the Church has the power of the Holy Spirit to overcome the world and the evil one. If we are going to win the battle, the Church must listen and trust God. It is time to walk in power and not in fear. Fear is of Satan; courage to proclaim the Gospel is from Jesus.

Jesus came for one reason only, to save the world from a lifetime of torment in Hell. It is time the Church had the courage to stand up against mediocrity, political correctness, compromise, and everything else the Church uses for an excuse. God demands that we stand. Today is the day; we can't wait any longer. Jesus says, "Fear Not! The angels have your back, but more than that, I have given you the power to walk in the Spirit; the power to conquer."